Ladies
of
the Lake

Do Fish Fart?

Answers to Kids' Questions About Lakes

SMILE GANG! WE'RE FAMOUS!

MALLARD DYNASTY

Text by Keltie Thomas
Illustrated by Deryk Ouseley

A FIREFLY BOOK

Published by Firefly Books Ltd. 2016
Copyright © 2016 Ontario Water Centre

First printing

Publisher Cataloging-in-Publication Data (U.S.)
Thomas, Keltie, 1966-, author.
Do fish fart? / Keltie Thomas.
Richmond Hill, Ontario, Canada : Firefly Books, 2016. Includes index.
Summary:"This book answers children's questions on the ecology of freshwater lakes, breaking down the science, plants, fish and animals, and geography of life underwater" — Provided by publisher.
ISBN 978-1-77085-727-8 (pbk.) ISBN 978-1-77085-728-5 (hardcover)
Lake ecology — Juvenile literature. Lake animals — Juvenile literature. Lake plants — Juvenile literature.
QH541.5.L3T566 |DDC 577.63 – dc23

Library and Archives Canada Cataloguing in Publication
Thomas, Keltie
[Do fish fart? (Firefly Books)]
Do fish fart? / Keltie Thomas.
Includes index.
ISBN 978-1-77085-728-5 (bound).—ISBN 978-1-77085-727-8 (paperback)
1. Freshwater ecology--Miscellanea--Juvenile literature. I. Title. II. Title: Do fish fart? (Firefly Books).
QH541.5.F7T56 2016   j577.6   C2015-908018-5

Published in the United States by
Firefly Books (U.S.) Inc.
P.O. Box 1338, Ellicott Station
Buffalo, New York 14205

Published in Canada by
Firefly Books Ltd.
50 Staples Avenue, Unit 1
Richmond Hill, Ontario L4B 0A7

Cover and interior design: Deryk Ouseley

Printed in Canada

The publisher gratefully acknowledges the financial support for our publishing program by the Government of Canada through the Canada Book Fund as administered by the Department of Canadian Heritage.

Contents

It's Your Water, Make a Splash!

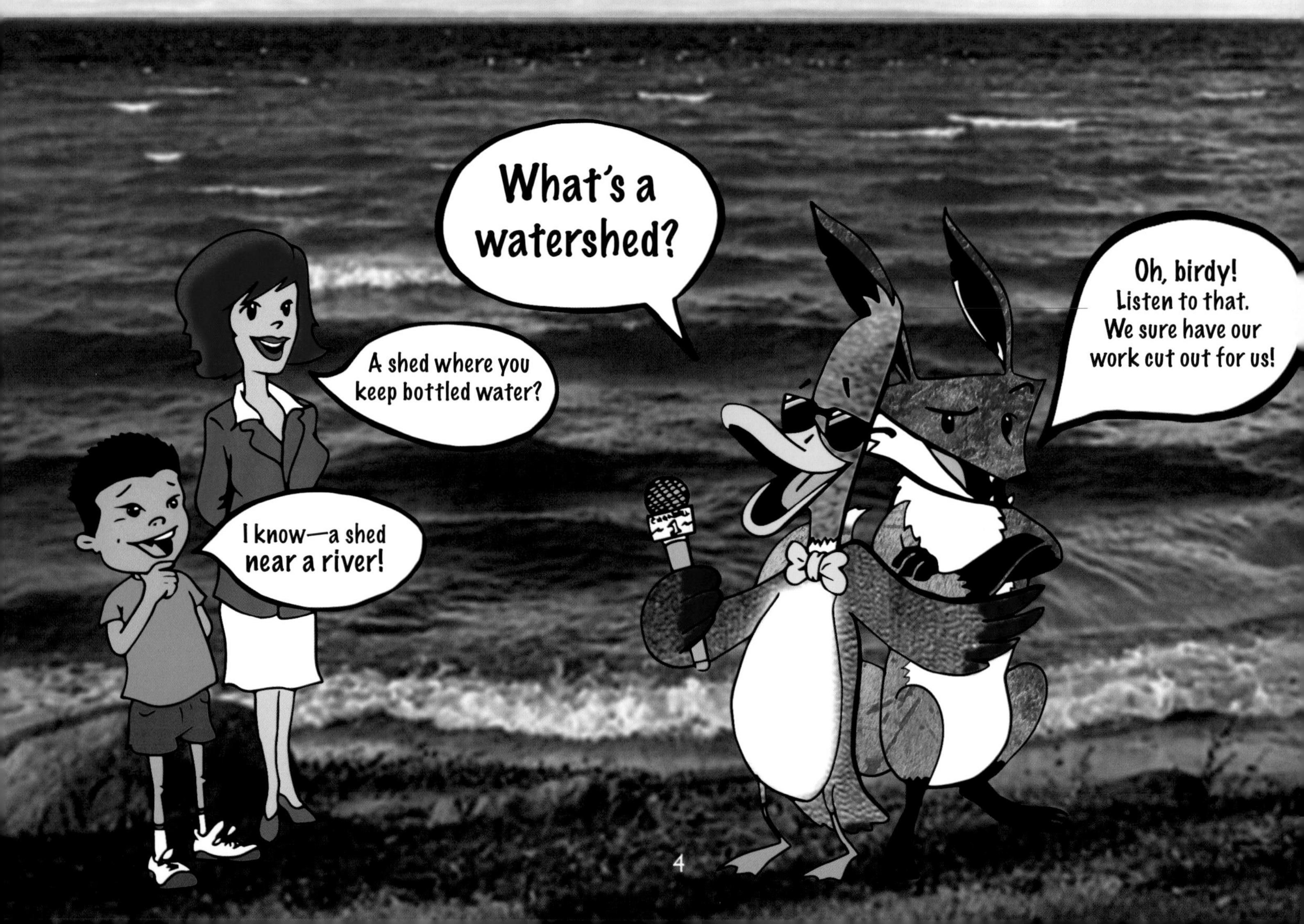

Have you ever seen a watershed? Think you could tell your BFF what exactly it is?

If your answer to one or both of these questions is "No," don't worry. You're not alone.

Not many people "get" what a watershed is, and some have some pretty wacky ideas. Just check out the scene left.

Did you know you may be sitting inside a watershed right now as you read this book?

In fact, you may know many many people who live in one. A watershed is like an enormous bathtub. It's an area of land where all the water drains into a lake, river or stream.

And what we all need to **"get"** about a watershed is this: what we do on the land in it affects the water in it.

For example, if we litter or use fertilizers to help our lawns, gardens and crops grow, they end up in the water. And when lots of trash, fertilizers and other things we use pile up in the lake, the water becomes unhealthy for plants and animals—including us.

The good news is that if we change what or how we do things in a watershed, we can help clean up our lakes and keep the water healthy. **How?** Read on, ask questions and look for answers. In this book, you'll find questions and answers that lots of kids in the Lake Simcoe watershed in southern Ontario asked about their lake. **So dive in and make a splash!**

Q & A with the Ladies of the Lake

Where did the title *Do Fish Fart?* come from?

That's the first question everyone asks! Many questions for this book were gathered at schools. At one school, two grade three kids asked "Do fish fart?" and they got hauled out of assembly for using foul language. This got us thinking. Since every question is important, maybe we should honor that by making *Do Fish Fart?* our title. And just wait till you see the answer on page 20!

Where did the questions in the book come from?

To get started, 2,100 kids at seven elementary schools and three libraries in the Lake Simcoe watershed came up with 3,000 questions. Then we spent weeks sorting and voting on the ones that would best help to tell the kids' story of water.

How did you get the answers?

We asked experts for help. You can see who they are on page 48. All the experts jumped right in. Some sent pictures, others wrote hundreds of words and they all had fun!!

Answers
to Your Burning Questions About
Our Lakes

Why is a lake not an ocean?

Oceans and lakes differ in size. Oceans are much, much larger than lakes. In fact, oceans cover about three-quarters of the Earth's surface. Oceans also contain lots of salt, whereas most lakes contain freshwater that humans can drink for survival.

LAKE WAVES CAN GET TOTALLY GNARLY SOMETIMES!

How do rivers form?

Got a source of water in a place where the land slopes? Then you've got what it takes to form a river. Once the glaciers that covered the Great Lakes area during the last ice age melted (see pages 8 and 9), meltwater and rainwater began to flow from high land to low land. Over time, the flowing water carved the surface of the land into the rivers, creeks and streams that drain into the Great Lakes today.

Does freshwater smell different from saltwater?

Fee-fi-fo-fum. I smell the salt of a big ocean… Do you recall that water has no odor at all? (See "Why Does Water Taste like Nothing?," page 11.) Thus, water smells only when something is in it. Because seawater has salt and might contain other minerals and things from its surrounding area, it has a smell unique to that area. However, freshwater that is 100% pure has no odor. But if freshwater contains dead trees, rotting weeds or the like, it will have a smell unique to those things. Pee-ew!

What if we run out of water? Will someone have invented a water substitute by then?

Predicting the future is a risky business. Just consider how often weather forecasters get it wrong. Water is unique. So far we have no substitute. But the water on Earth naturally recycles itself, so our best bet for the future is to use water wisely. Waste not, want not, dude!

Why are lakes blue but water is clear in a glass when we drink it?

Sure, water has no color, but sometimes it looks blue thanks to light. White light like sunlight is made of red, orange, yellow, green and blue light. Water doesn't absorb blue and green light as well as the others. Water's surface scatters and reflects blue and green light, and this makes lakes look blue. And the bigger the body of water, the bluer it looks. What's more, sometimes a lake appears blue because its surface reflects the color of the sky. But in a glass, water looks clear. That's because its surface isn't big enough to reflect enough blue light to look blue.

That Was Then!

How did water first get to the Great Lakes?

Say you could hop in a time machine and travel back to the last ice age. You'd come across glaciers that covered the area where the Great Lakes are today. In some places, these huge sheets of ice were a whopping 2 miles (3 km) thick. When the Earth's climate warmed up about 20,000 years ago, the glaciers began to move north and melt. As the thick, heavy ice sheets moved, they scraped the land, digging out large basins. What's more, as the ice melted, the melt water filled the basins, and that's how glaciers brought water to the Great Lakes.

THERE SURE WASN'T A SHORTAGE OF ICE BACK THEN!

This Is Now!

How did glaciers bring water to the Great Lakes?

Look at the drawings below of southern Ontario from the last ice age to 4,000 years ago. Then see if you can place them in the correct order on the timeline. (Answer is at right.)

Snapshots in Time

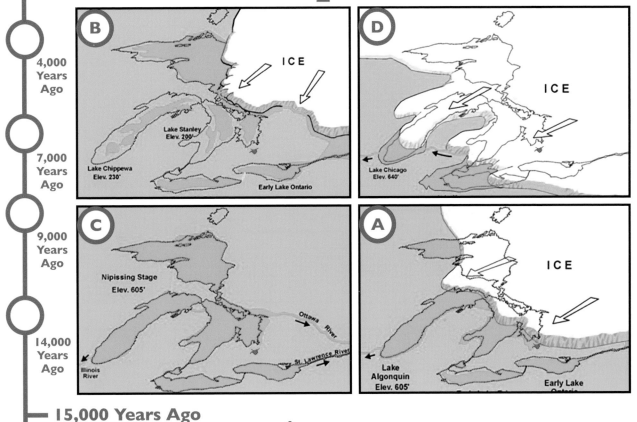

Present Day

4,000 Years Ago

7,000 Years Ago

9,000 Years Ago

14,000 Years Ago

15,000 Years Ago

B — ICE — Lake Stanley Elev. 200' — Lake Chippewa Elev. 230' — Early Lake Ontario

D — ICE — Lake Chicago Elev. 640'

C — Nipissing Stage Elev. 605' — Ottawa River — Illinois River — St. Lawrence River

A — ICE — Lake Algonquin Elev. 605' — Early Lake Ontario

Answers: 14,000 years ago = D, 9,000 years ago = A, 7,000 years ago = B, 4,000 years ago = C

9

Answers
to Your Burning
Questions About
Water

Why is water wet?

Because it's water?! No, seriously though, water is wet when it's a liquid rather than a gas or a solid. All liquids are wet. We use the word "wet" to describe our experience with liquids. In particular, we use "wet" to describe what water feels like. When water touches us and flows over our skin, we say we got wet. Likewise, when we say something is wet, we mean that it is covered or soaked with water.

QUESTIONS OF THE WEIRD

Could we get scoops of snow, put them in a filter pitcher and drink it?

Not if you want water that's safe to drink. Like rainwater, snow can pick up harmful bacteria, dust and even the odd insect wing as it falls from the sky. What's more, once snow is on the ground it can pick up road salt as well as animal urine and feces. Water filter systems like a Brita aren't designed to filter out these things and disinfect water. They're made to filter treated water that's already safe to drink to make it better by removing things such as chlorine.

Is fluoride in our drinking water a bad thing?

Fluoride is a natural mineral found in groundwater and the environment. It's often added to drinking water during the treatment process because it helps prevent tooth decay. Drinking water is tested to check that the amount of fluoride is safe to drink.

Why does it matter if I leave a tap running?

Drip, drip, drip! A running tap wastes a lot of water —and not just any old water. That's tap water that has taken a lot of people, time and electricity to clean and treat so it's safe for you to drink. What's more, once tap water goes down the drain, it goes to a water pollution control plant to be cleaned before going back into the lake. So don't be a drip. Use water wisely. It's too precious to waste!

Why does water taste like nothing?

Water has no color, no odor and no taste, but your tongue has taste buds that detect salty, sweet, sour and bitter flavors. Since pure water has none of these flavors to detect, you taste nothing. The only time water has a flavor is when something has been added to it, such as drink mix or metal runoff from pipes. Then you taste whatever has been added—not water! Sometimes land and climate can change water's taste or smell. In fact, humans and other animals can tell if water is too salty or putrid to drink from its taste or smell.

ANSWERS
to Your Burning Questions About

Did the water on Earth come from space?

Yep. Scientists think water hitchhiked a ride with comets, asteroids or meteorites that landed on Earth or that Earth picked up water on a jaunt around the sun (see "How Did Water Get on Earth?" at right).

When was water formed?

Ever heard of the Big Bang? If not, you will. Scientists think this explosion gave birth to our universe almost 14 billion years ago. In the early days after the Big Bang, hydrogen, the most plentiful chemical in the universe, formed.

Later, when stars were born, oxygen, the third-most plentiful chemical in the universe, formed. As the stars died, they exploded, blasting oxygen into space. In pockets of the universe where the temperature and pressure were just right, hydrogen and oxygen joined, forming water.

How did water get on Earth?

Wouldn't you, scientists and the whole wide world like to know?! About nine billion years after the universe was born, scientists think that swirling clouds of gas and dust clumped together to form planets. Water was part of the clouds that formed Earth, but it didn't stick around for long. Scientists think hot temperatures on early Earth vaporized it. The water vapor then floated away as early Earth had no gaseous envelope like the present-day atmosphere to bounce the vapor back.

Some scientists think that comets, meteorites or asteroids might have brought water to Earth later. Others think that Earth might have picked up water from thick clouds of gas and dust, called solar nebulae, that it passed through on one of its journeys around the sun. It is still a mystery!

Did you know that over **seven billion** people on Earth all depend on **freshwater** to live. That doesn't even include what the other animals **need!**

12

Water

What is water?

Water is a big part of you. About two-thirds of your body is water. Water is the stuff of life. Not only you but all humans and living creatures are made of water.

A drop of water is made of billions of water molecules. In turn, each water molecule is made of two hydrogen atoms and one oxygen atom (shown above). Atoms are the tiny building blocks of all matter in the universe. They are so small that they are invisible to the naked eye!

What would the world look like with no water?

Astronauts and anybody else out there could say goodbye to the blue-green marble they gaze at in the sky. Gone would be the deep blue seas and puffy white rain clouds. Gone too would be the lush green forests and all other life-forms.

Before water flowed over the Earth, carving out riverbeds and filling up ocean basins, the planet was a rocky molten hot spot devoid of all life. Fiery showers of hot lava spewed out of volcanoes and flowed all over. To anybody who might have been somewhere out there, the world likely looked like a great ball of fire.

How much freshwater is still left on Earth?

Believe it or not, the amount of freshwater on our planet has stayed nearly the same over time. That's because Earth's atmosphere—a thin layer of gases around the planet—constantly recycles water back into our "cup."

Even though water covers more than two-thirds of our planet, very little of it is freshwater. If you could pour all the water on Earth into 100 cups, salty ocean water would fill 97 cups and freshwater only three. What's more, only a few drops of those three cups would be readily available for you to drink and use as most of Earth's freshwater is in the ground or trapped in glaciers.

Earth has about 22,339 cubic miles (93,111 km^3) of freshwater that's easily available from lakes, rivers and streams. That's more than enough to fill the Great Lakes four times!

Answers
to Your Burning Questions About
Rock Bottom
Stuff

What's on the bottom of a lake?

If you went scuba diving at the bottom of a lake, you'd see that it's made of a variety of sands, silts, mud and rock deposits. You'd also come across logs, remains of dead plants and animals and remains of whatever objects people have lost or thrown into the lake.

When you build a sand castle, the sand doesn't hold any water. So how does sand hold all that water?

Sand gets by with a little help from its friends—silt, clay, mud and rock. No kidding! Tightly packed layers of silt, clay and mud lie below the sand at the bottom of lakes. These dense layers help stop water from moving. Deeper still, layers of rock, such as shale, limestone and granite, also help out. This bedrock stops water from moving down and running out of the lake.

Are there any shipwrecks in the Great Lakes?

Loads! There's even an entire museum devoted to them. The Great Lakes Shipwreck Museum estimates that there are 6,000 known shipwrecks in the Great Lakes, and there might be more we don't know about. The Great Lakes are the biggest group of freshwater lakes on Earth. In fact, they have rolling waves, constant winds, strong currents and mighty depths much like seas. Is it any wonder so many ships have been wrecked there? One of the most famous is the *Edmund Fitzgerald*. Not only did the ship have up-to-date safety equipment when it sank in 1975, but it also vanished from the radar screens that were tracking it. No one knows why it sank and none of the crew survived.

ANOTHER DAY IN SCUBA PARADISE!

Answers
to Your Burning Questions About
Fish

Great Lakes

How did fish get into lakes?

Once the glaciers of the last ice age melted away, or so the theory goes, fish came from far and near. Many fish species migrated through rivers and lakes from warm waters in the south. Others may have come from places further away. For example, the eggs of some species may have hitched a ride on the feet or bills of birds or other animals. Still others may have hitchhiked with indigenous peoples who hunted, fished or lived near the lake.

Do fish get affected by bad weather?

Yup! Fish are cold-blooded creatures that can be affected by weather and changes in water temperature. For example, if summer temperatures stay warm, around 77°F (25°C), for several weeks, fish might actively feed the entire time. However, if the weather suddenly turns cold and the water temperature drops to 59°F (15°C), bass and similar fish usually become sluggish and less active, so they might eat less until they become used to the cooler water temperature.

How can fish survive in the winter? And if they die, why are there still so many of them?

Sure many lakes freeze over, but the water below the ice remains above the freezing point. That's why fish don't turn into Popsicles in the winter. What's more, fish are cold-blooded. This means their body temperature varies with the temperature of the water. Therefore, fish don't feel the cold like warm-blooded creatures, such as humans, and they don't die off in winter. Some fish like minnows have short lives. Others, such as lake trout, have long lives. Eventually all fish die, but never all at once. As adult fish reproduce, their offspring grow and reproduce to replace older fish that die. And so the fishy cycle of life turns out plenty of fish!

Do fish bite you?

Fish aren't fussy when it comes to food. Almost anything will do for a quick bite. But many fish—sunfish, rock bass, perch, smallmouth bass and largemouth bass—have teeth more like sandpaper than teeth. Therefore, anglers can safely hold the fish by the lower jaw without getting bit. On the other hand, pike, muskie and walleye do have teeth that can sink into you, so it's best not to hold them by the mouth and to keep your fingers clear of the mouth. Although these fish won't nip at you, their teeth can be sharp enough to cut you.

Why do fish have to be in water?

Quick. Think fast: why do people have to be in air? To breathe, right? Water is to fish a lot like air is to people. Fish live in water and breathe with special organs called gills. Gills are usually red and can be seen below a fish's "cheeks." They are amazing organs that help fish breathe oxygen held in water. If people had gills, we might be able to breathe underwater, too!

If people had gills, we might be able to breathe underwater, too!

Can fish drown?

Even natural-born swimmers like fish drown sometimes. If a fish's gills stop working, for example, not enough oxygen can reach its brain and it might drown. Also, if water is extremely low in oxygen, or has no oxygen at all, fish can't breathe. The result? They drown. The same thing happens when you take a fish out of water for too long. The fish can't breathe and eventually kicks the bucket.

Do fish impact the cleanliness of lakes?

Not really. The poop and pee of fish decompose, or break down, naturally. And when fish die, their flesh decomposes or is gobbled up by other fish or crustaceans, such as crayfish. On the other hand, live, healthy fish can be a sign that a lake is clean and healthy, too.

Why do fish smell?

Whether you want to know why fish stink or why fish sniff the world around them, we've got you covered. First off, some fish don't stink much at all, but others have distinctive odors. Some people say the lake whitefish smells like a cucumber! The government even has trained dogs that sniff out fish to help catch poachers. Secondly, fish use their sense of smell to find food. For example, when anglers use worms as bait for sunfish, the sunfish often smell the worm before they see it.

Sniff Sniff

Do fish fart?

You bet they do—and how! The lake herring, or cisco, in the Great Lakes may even communicate with each other by farting. Many fish have an air bladder that contains gas that helps them stay afloat. In cisco, the air bladder is connected to an anal opening, and cisco often release gas through the anal opening when they are scared and when they move up or down in the water column. The toots might tell other fish where they're at. Have you ever communicated by farting?

Hi Frank, how are you?

Doing great Bob. Thanks for asking!

Gills
(shown through skin)

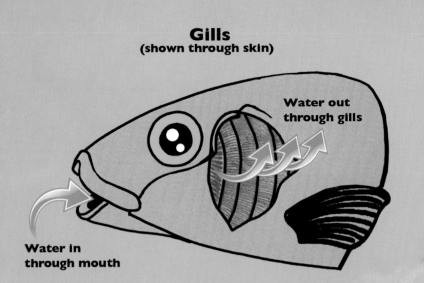

Water out through gills

Water in through mouth

Do fish drink water?

Not like you and the rest of us humans. However, water constantly flows through their mouths and the gills on either side of their throats. Fish breathe through their gills, which take in oxygen from the water.

Pop Drop

The less fish hatchlings move, the more energy from the yolk sac they have to develop fins and the rest of their bodies.

What do fish eat?

Fish aren't picky eaters. What's for dinner depends on which kind of fish are dining, their age and the "catch of the day." When fish first hatch, they eat from a yolk sac. This is a small amount of food that they're born with in their belly. Once they finish off the yolk sac, fish eat tiny plants and animals called phytoplankton and zooplankton. As fish grow, their mouths get bigger and they can eat bigger and bigger things—from tiny insects to other fish. Eventually, some fish even eat shellfish and small aquatic animals. When they're on the hunt for a bite, adult fish'll eat whatever meal swims by.

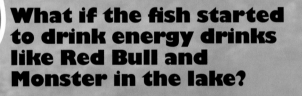

QUESTIONS OF THE WEIRD

What if the fish started to drink energy drinks like Red Bull and Monster in the lake?

Well… they would have lots of energy… maybe even enough to make a speedy getaway from any monsters like Champ or Igopogo (see "Do Monsters Live in Lakes?" on page 38.) Seriously though, did you know that what we drink can eventually end up in our lakes? That's because cleaned sewer water empties into lakes. Even though sewage treatment facilities remove harmful chemicals from the water, tiny amounts of some chemicals, such as caffeine, remain. Researchers from Lakehead University in Orillia, Canada, discovered traces of caffeine in lake water. They don't think these traces will have a drastic effect on fish, but the long-term effects of sipping the dregs of Red Bull, Monster, and other caffeine-energy drinks aren't known yet.

Why are some fish ugly?

Just like beauty, ugliness is all in the eye of the beholder. All fish have fins and a tail. However, these parts and other physical traits can vary based on the environment where fish live. For example, fish that live where lots of water plants grow may have a different body shape and coloring than those that live in open water. Their shape and coloring may help them blend in with their surroundings to avoid predators. Also, fish that live in fast-flowing water may have more streamlined bodies and fins than those that dwell in open water to help them get around effectively.

Check out Third Eye Louie's extra eye!

Are there three-eyed fish?

Third Eye Louie caused a stir when he popped up in Lake Nipissing in northern Ontario in 2014. Some people thought the three-eyed walleye had developed an extra eye due to a nuclear spill. Others thought sewage pollution and algae blooms were to blame. Other scientists thought a mutation in the fish's genes—information passed on from the fish's parents that determines its traits and how its body develops and works—was the culprit. Though reports of three-eyed fish like this turn up every now and then, chances are you won't run into one at your local swimming hole.

Here's lookin' at you kid!

Pop Drop

Fish have faint lines on their tails, from their gills to their tail. These lines sense movement and vibrations in the water, so fish can detect predators and prey and can avoid crashing into one another.

22

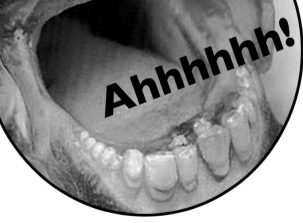

Say ahhh...

Ahhhhhh!

Is there a fish that looks like a human?

Not in the real world. But in 2014, a Russian angler caught a fish that had human-like teeth. When experts examined the unusual catch, they thought the fish was a piranha. How's that for getting a bite? What's more, the pacu, a South American freshwater fish, also has human-like pearly whites. Though a few have been spotted in North American lakes, experts say the tropical fish won't survive the winter.

Check out these pearly whites! The South American pacu fish has teeth that look like human teeth!

Do fish vomit?

Hurl, barf or retch. Whatever you want to call it, fish do vomit. Every now and then, anglers see a fish that they've just landed throw up smaller fish that the fish has just eaten.

23

How do fish have babies? Do they look after them?

Some fish do a whole song and dance—a.k.a. a ritual. When bass spawn, for example, a male fish builds a nest with his tail. He gently nudges a female toward the nest, coaxing her to swim overtop and lay eggs. The male then fertilizes the eggs with sperm. The female takes off, and the male sticks around to guard the eggs from predators, such as round gobies and beetles.

After three to five days, the eggs hatch, and the male bass is a single dad. For the next month, he doesn't go anywhere. He doesn't eat. He spends all his time and energy protecting the hatchlings and ensuring their survival. But most fish species aren't devoted parents like that. They don't build nests, and they don't watch over their young.

Pop Drop

In yellow perch, the female lays lots of eggs on the bottom of a lake, the male fertilizes the eggs, and then they take off. They leave the eggs to hatch on their own. The sheer number of eggs ensures that enough yellow perch survive for the next generation.

How smart are fish?

Some people say fish are not very smart at all because most have a brain even smaller than a pea. However, fish are smart enough to capture their own food, escape from predators and spawn successfully. But some fish don't have smarts, or instincts, as finely tuned as others. Those ones may be the first to perish, becoming living, er dead, proof of the survival of the fittest law that rules lakes.

WHO ARE YOU CALLING A PEA BRAIN?!

How do fish communicate with other fish?

Toot! Toot! Hey kid, I'm talking to you. Scientists think some fish communicate by farting (see "Do Fish Fart?," page 20). These fish make sounds by blowing gas out of an anal opening connected to their air bladder. However, most fish don't have this ability. But a number make sounds like grunts, chirps and pops to attract a mate, scare away predators and get their bearings.

How do fish have sex?

Fish swim, wriggle and squirm, but the average Joe and Joelle Fish don't have sex at all. Sound fishy? Fish reproduce, or have young, by spawning, not by having sex. A female fish lays eggs then a male fish swims above the eggs and fertilizes them. Sharks and rays are another kettle of fish though, as they do have sex to reproduce. For example, a male shark puts a clasper, an organ on his back fin, inside a female shark. His clasper then releases sperm to fertilize eggs inside the female shark's body. However, most sharks and rays live in oceans, not lakes.

Answers
to Your Burning Questions About
Poo and Pee

Do fish urinate? And if they do, when we go swimming are we swimming in fish pee?

Fish gotta swim and fish gotta pee, so if you swim in a lake, you do swim in fish pee and poo. But it's nothing to wrinkle your nose or moan "eww" about. This fish waste occurs naturally in the water and becomes so diluted, or thin and weak, that it doesn't pose any danger to people's health.

Do fish pollute by peeing and pooping?

Here's the scoop. Like all animals, fish do pee and poo. Fish release their organic matter naturally, adding nutrients to the lakes that aquatic plants and other organisms can feed on. So their pee and poo adds to the cycle of life within the wonderful underwater world of a lake. And that's the scoop on poop!

Pop Drop

The Great Lakes provide drinking water for some 40 million people. The lake water is treated to make it clean and safe to drink.

When you go to the washroom, where does it go?

All the water you flush down the toilet, including any solid and liquid matter in it, ends up at a water pollution control plant. The wastewater gets cleaned at the plant before it's allowed back into our lakes and rivers.

🐟 ➡ 💩 + 💧 = OK!

Is it OK to pee in a lake?

Remember that lakes are home to many creatures. Plants, fish and other animals all live in the water. Plus, you and your friends, and many other people, swim in the lake. So if millions of people peed in the lake it wouldn't be a good thing. Help keep the lake clean for the fish, other animals, plants and swimmers by using a toilet. By showing our respect and love for the water, we help our lakes.

27

Answers
to Your Burning Questions About
Dumping

Why do people throw shopping carts, sofas and other stuff into the water?

It all boils down to this: they don't have a special relationship with the water. Without this relationship, people don't care about the water and the water is just another dumping ground.

Not caring is contagious, and once one person dumps stuff in the water, other people dump there too. The good news is that caring is also contagious. Once people connect with a lake in fun and inspiring ways, they fall back in love with the water. Then they want to protect it, not harm it.

What if we dumped a bomb into a lake?

Ka-boom! If the bomb went off, the explosion would kill plants, animals and people in the water. It could also damage the shoreline and make the water and shoreline radioactive. Exposure to radiation can make plants, animals and people sick. So depending on the reach of the blast, plants, animals and people in the surrounding area could die or become sick as well. People would also likely avoid the lake. This would cut down on recreation, an important industry for many lakeside communities. People could lose jobs, and the communities could fall on hard times. What's more, radiation contamination and other effects of the bomb would affect the lake for years.

What if someone threw a bag of candy into a lake?

Fish might get tooth decay and birds might crash and burn on the sugar… Just kidding! Most likely the candy would dissolve, or break down, in the lake because it's made of ingredients safe for people to eat. The bag would be another story though, especially if it was plastic. Plastic does not break down readily. Plastic bags have been known to float around the ocean for a year or more before they break down. And when they do, they release toxic chemicals that can wash up on shore or be absorbed by fish—and us if we eat the fish.

Questions of the Weird

What if everyone poured drink mix into a lake?

Drink mix isn't good for fish and other animals. Pouring a little bit of drink mix in a lake is like peeing a little bit in a lake. Even though little bits of it might not hurt the fish and other animals, lots of drink mix could make them very sick. Plus, it might kill off the plants in the lake.

29

What if a shark was dropped into a lake?

Chances are Jaws wouldn't last long. Most sharks require saltwater to live, not freshwater, like most lake water. Sharks evolved in saltwater and have very salty bodies. Sharks undergo osmosis in water. During osmosis, water moves through a membrane from a less salty area to a more salty area to even out the salt concentration on both sides of the membrane. So water would move from the lake into the shark's body—so much water that the shark might burst!

DON'T MESS WITH ME, SHARKIE.

What would happen if I threw a tire into a lake?

Tires are made of oil and other chemicals. Many of these chemicals are harmful to waterfowl, other wildlife and the environment. As the tire slowly breaks down, or decomposes, it would release these chemicals into the water. The chemicals could then harm the environment and wildlife.

What would happen if you put thousands of bugs into a lake?

Bugs that fly, bugs that swim or bugs that crawl? It would depend on the kind of bugs. Unless they were water bugs, they'd most likely be eaten by fish or drown.

Where do drugs go if I put them into the water?

If you put drugs down the drain, in the toilet or even in the garbage, they end up in rivers, lakes, drinking water and soil. Researchers have found traces of medications, other medicinal drugs and personal care products like shampoo in all of these places. Therefore, we need to dispose of drugs safely to protect our drinking water and ecosystem. Many drug stores accept unused medications to do just that.

DOES ANYONE HAVE SOME SALT?

Pop Drop

Freshwater sharks take in a lot more water than saltwater sharks, so much so that they pee 20 times more than saltwater sharks.

Answers
to Your Burning Questions About
Gooey Green Stuff

What is all the green gooey, squishy stuff on the top of a lake?

It's not slime. It's not ooze. And much to everyone's relief, it's not even mutant! In the spring, mats of dead aquatic plants might float on top of a lake until they wash up on shore or sink. These dead plants help fuel the natural cycle that reuses nutrients and energy in a lake.

Pop Drop
As zebra mussels eat, they filter nutrients out of water. Each one filters 1 quart (1 L) a day!

Zebra Mussels
Zebra mussels aren't good news. They are an invasive species that crowds out native mussels and clams that are part of the balanced ecosystem. Their waste also contains nutrients that increase the growth of weeds in lakes.

What if the fish eat the green stuff? Is that OK?

What's food for one species may look questionable to another, especially us humans. Even different species of fish have different food sources. Some fish nibble on the aquatic plants that make up the green stuff. Others gobble up tiny insects that live on these floating plants.

Why is there so much algae?

There's so much of the bloomin' stuff, the lake is green! Algae bloom like crazy when there's oodles of phosphorus, lots of sunlight, and warm water temperatures. Phosphorus is a nutrient. High levels of it can get into lakes from fertilizers that we use to grow crops and plants as well as household cleaning products. The good news is that zebra mussels feed on green algae, filtering the water as they gobble up gobs of the stuff. The bad news is that zebra mussels don't like blue-green algae, which blooms around the Great Lakes. Some blue-green algae blooms are toxic for animals, including us, and they make water unsafe for swimming, boating and drinking.

What if we drank the messy green water? Would we die?

Drinking water straight out of a lake is a no-no. No ifs, ands or buts about it. Even if the lake water is not messy and green but clean and clear, it contains small amounts of bacteria and algae that can make you sick. Drinking it can lead to nausea, vomiting, diarrhea and, in rare cases, even death. However, we have water treatment plants that make lake water safe for drinking. And once the water has been treated, there's no better thirst quencher. In fact, the Great Lakes provide drinking water for 40 million people.

Algae I.Q. Test

Read the Q & As on this page. Then take the quiz below to check your algae I.Q. (See answers below.)

1. How do you decrease the amount of algae in a lake?

a) Invite zebra mussels for dinner

b) Reduce the amount of phosphorus in fertilizers, household cleaners and other products

c) Both of the above

2. I'm scared of algae. Should I be?

a) Yes

b) No

c) Both of the above

3. Where is the green slime spot on a lake?

a) On the surface

b) At the bottom

c) Where all the algae hang out

Algae I.Q. Test Answers:

Q1 = B

Q2 = C (Some algae blooms are toxic, but by cutting down the phosphorus in products, we can reduce these blooms)

Q3 = A

Your Algae I.Q.:

If you got 3/3, you know the difference between the green gooey stuff and algae and what keeps algae in check.

If you got 2/3, you're learning to separate the algae facts from fiction.

If you got 1/3, you need to work on seeing the algae through the weeds.

If you got 0/3, read the Q & As on the page again and give yourself a do-over.

Answers
to Your Burning
Questions About
Plants and Trees

Do forests help the water or does water help the forests?

They're like BFFs! Check out how the water and forests take care of each other.

Water Cleans the Forest

Ever stand under a tree when it was raining really hard? Did you notice that you didn't get as wet as those not under the tree? That's because trees catch water on their leaves. The water then drips slowly from leaf to leaf long after the rain stops. This gives the trees a shower. That's a good thing because trees get dirty just like you. The dripping water cleans the leaves, washing dirt out of openings on the underside that trees "breathe" through.

The Forest Helps the Lake

Fast-moving water is strong. It can move dirt, rocks and gravel. But as trees catch rain, they slow the water down. This cuts down the water's strength, so it doesn't wash away the soil under the trees. It also gives the water more time to sink into the ground, where trees and other forest plants need it to drink. What's more, the roots of the trees and plants grip the soil and help hold it in place. If they didn't, the water would carry the soil into the lake. Then the soil could smother fish eggs, which are laid close to shore. Eventually, fish might no longer hatch in the lake. So when forests catch water and stop soil from getting away, they help the lake.

Why Do Plants Need Water?

Just call it survival of the wettest. Plants are living things, and all living things need water to stay alive. But plants need more than most. That's because plants contain and use more water. Plants are made of 90% water. They absorb water through their roots. The water then travels up the stem to the leaves, where plants use it to make sugar for energy. It also provides pressure that helps the stem stand tall and the leaves stay firm. If plants don't get enough water, the pressure drops and they wilt!

Pop Drop

Big birds nest in big trees. If we cut down all of our big trees, we wouldn't see the great blue heron along our lakeshores anymore.

Pop Quiz!

How do plants help the lake?
Let us count the ways!

Plants provide:

1. Shelter. Fish hide among aquatic plants to get out of the sun, to avoid predators or to ambush prey.

2. Safe areas for fish to lay eggs and young fish to grow and develop.

3. The "breath of life." Plants release oxygen in the water, which fish and other organisms need to breathe.

4. A natural water filter. Plants along the water's edge slow down, filter, clean and purify the water that drains into the lake from nearby land.

5. Stability. Plants hold soil along the water's edge so it doesn't wash away, which would make the water muddy and less healthy for fish and other aquatic organisms.

What can I do to help the lake?

First, get yourself a spoon and fill it with water. Look at your spoonful of water and think about all the things that water does to help you. You can't survive without it. Seeing a lake or a river can make you feel happy or special or small or even big. Poking a toe into a little puddle where bugs are swimming connects you to the wacky and wonderful world of water you live in. That's all you really have to do—treat the lake like one of your best friends. Now what will you do with your spoonful of water?

Answers
to Your Burning Questions About
Animals

Which animals hang out at the Great Lakes?

Ever seen a Blanding's turtle, Jefferson salamander or American eel? All three of these rare species live in the Great Lakes watershed. You might not spot many though, because so few still exist that the survival of their species is at risk. Many not-so-rare species hang out at the Great Lakes, too. If you keep your eyes peeled, you might see a moose on the loose. You might also spot a beaver, river otter, gray wolf, coyote, Canada lynx or little brown bat. And chances are you won't have to look far to see one of the many birds that hang out there. Bald eagles, loons, cormorants and many others feed, breed and rest at the Great Lakes. In fact, millions of birds drop by the lakes every spring and fall as they migrate between their winter and summer digs.

The Blanding's Turtle

What happens when a cat tries to eat a fish?

That depends if the fish is alive or dead! A cat may play with a live small fish before ever trying to eat it, just like playing with a mouse. But if the fish is dead, a cat may make a meal of it. After all, it's no secret that cats love to eat fish!

Can beavers build a dam in the middle of a lake?

Beavers are top-notch construction workers. No doubt about it. They cut down trees for timber with their powerful front teeth. They carry the timber between their teeth along with mud and stones in their forepaws to a building site. Then they use these materials to build through the night. But even if they could dam in the middle of a lake, they probably wouldn't. Beavers build dams on rivers and streams to hold back water. This creates a deep pond where they can build homes, called lodges, for easy access to food during the winter. So look out for signs of beavers at work on the streams and rivers around lakes.

Why are zebra mussels called that?

Zebra mussels get their name from the pattern of dark and light stripes on their shells that looks like the stripes of a zebra. But not all zebra mussels have stripes. Some are entirely dark or light. Zebra mussels and their cousins, quagga mussels, are invasive species to North America, and we all need to be careful to stop them from spreading to other water bodies. Thus, it's important to check for zebra mussels that could be stuck to your boat or trailer whenever you move from one water body to another. Tiny mussel babies called "veligers" can also stick to boats or float in the water in a boat's bilge! So be sure to clean and drain dry your boat and trailer too.

Answers to Your Burning Questions About Monsters

What if there is a monster in a lake?

What if, indeed! Some lakes are remnants of ancient lakes that were much bigger long ago. Those ancient lakes might have had all kinds of fish that we might call monsters, especially if they looked anything like the weird-looking fish that live deep in the ocean today. The frilled-shark, for example, is a "living fossil" that has many physical characteristics of its ancestors who swam the seas in the time of the dinosaurs.

Other ocean-going creeps of the deep include the scary-looking anglerfish, the freaky fangtooth, the Pacific viperfish, whose jagged needlelike teeth are too big to allow it to close its mouth, the vampire squid and the wolffish, who crushes mollusks, shellfish and sea urchins with its jaws.

Are there any man-eating fish in the Great Lakes?

Got visions of Jaws swimming in your head? Relax. Unlike the oceans, the Great Lakes are not home to sharks or other predatory fish that might eat humans. The Great Lakes are a freshwater environment, and most predators like those at the top of the food chain live only in saltwater. Phew!

What if Godzilla put 500 pieces of garbage in the lake?

Local police might have a monster of a problem trying to get Godzilla to stop. But 500 kids could get together and clean up the garbage in just one day and even build a few

Do monsters live in lakes?

Legend has it that a monster named Champ lives in Lake Champlain in New York. Stories also surface that a monster named Igopogo lives in Lake Simcoe in Ontario. Some people say its name comes from Ogopogo, a legendary monster in Lake Okanagan in British Columbia.

Igopogo has a head like a dog and has been spotted basking in the sun, or so the legend goes. But no hard evidence has been found to prove that any of these monsters exist in the world beyond myth and legend.

Igopogo or what? That's what these kids wondered as they looked at the humps that surfaced on Lake Simcoe in 1976. And it's still a question people ask today.

Did Bigfoot ever go for a swim in the Great Lakes?

No one knows for sure. No hard evidence, such as teeth or bones, has ever been found to prove if Bigfoot exists—let alone where the monster might hang out and

The anglerfish lures its prey with a tentacle attached to its head that emits light. Its victim never sees the danger just inches away!

Pacific Viper Fish

Fangtooth

Vampire Squid

Answers
to Your Burning Questions About
Pollution

Do animals pollute or affect how clean the water is? Or is it just people who pollute?

Hey, did you see that three-eyed fish?

Yeah! It must be some kind of mutant weirdo!

Pop Drop

Do big speedboats pollute more than small ones? Size doesn't matter. All boaters need to make sure they don't pollute by ensuring their motor is always in good working order.

Are there mutant animals in lakes from pollution?

No mutant ninja creatures bent on taking over the world have turned up…yet. But many forms of pollution can end up in lakes, including drugs, medicine, and chemicals that people have dumped down toilets. And they can have lasting and devastating effects on the diverse inhabitants of lakes. Frogs, fish, waterfowl, and even us humans rely on clean water to live.

Where does the oil and gas on the boat go?

As a boat engine runs, it emits fumes from oil and gas into the air. These fumes are known as emissions. Emissions can damage our air, land and water. Cutting down on emissions cuts down their effect on the environment. Boat engines in good working order have fewer emissions than those in poor working order. They also are less likely to leak oil and gas into the water, which is never good. Thus, taking care of your boat engine can help take care of the environment.

All animals—wild animals, party animals and regular ol' humans—pollute our environment a bit. Our bodies release waste that has *E. coli* bacteria in it. *E. coli* are tiny organisms that live in our gut to make vitamins and stop harmful bacteria from invading our bodies.

But if pet waste is disposed of incorrectly or if human waste from faulty septic systems or, in rare cases, from sewage treatment plants leach into the soil, heavy rain can wash *E. coli* into streams and down into lakes. Most *E. coli* are harmless, but some types can cause disease. That's why we need to be careful about what we let into our water.

Does the water get dirty from boats?

Yep. Boats should be washed, drained and dried before going out on the water. This will help keep out things like gas, oil and small creatures that don't belong in lakes.

If we pour soap in a lake, will it become a bubble bath?

Not in your wildest dreams! Bubble bath has a special chemical that makes it bubble and foam. Soap eventually breaks down in water, splitting into the chemicals that it's made from. One of these is phosphorus. So if you pour lots of soap into a lake, the phosphorus levels will rise. In turn, plant growth will increase, cutting off oxygen for fish and destroying places where fish can live.

QUESTIONS OF THE WEIRD

How long does it take for a lake to get polluted?

Well, without trying to beat around the bush, or the lake, it depends. Here's why. A lake is polluted when a person, organism or thing can no longer use it as usual. How long it takes for this to happen depends on many things that vary, such as the size of the lake, the type of pollutant and the amount of pollutant. For example, a little gasoline can have a huge effect on water quality, but phosphorus doesn't affect the water quality much unless there's a ton of it. The land and streams around the lake also affect how long it takes to get polluted. If many of the streams draining into the lake are contaminated, they can pollute it quickly.

How can water pollution happen so fast?

Believe it or not, rivers and lakes can bear pollution up to a point without showing signs of trouble. But once the pollution rises above this point, the effects of contamination rise rapidly. Aquatic plants and algae begin to grow out of control, choking up the rivers and lakes and using up precious oxygen. The result? Fish die, the water tastes and smells bad, bacteria multiply and the water turns cloudy. Major pollution like this comes from waste created by the uncontrolled growth of cities and the development of housing, industries, highways or natural resources. If we give more thought to how to control this waste before such development takes place, we might be able to limit the amount of waste based on the health of the lakes. And if we continue to develop based on money rather than the environment, we are brewing disaster for both our lakes and ourselves.

How can we get it all clean, the rivers and the lakes?

All of us—people like you and me, corporations, businesses and cities—need to work together. Follow the numbers below to see the big picture of what we need to do.

1 Meet the Rockin' Duo!

Nutrients in nature like P and N (phosphates and nitrates) are fantastic at helping all living things grow. But when people allow a whole bunch of these good guys to get into a lake, they turn into bad guys. And the bad guys can really rock and wreck the lake.

2 How do P and N wreck lakes?

They fertilize aquatic plants, so the plants grow like crazy. They also cause algae blooms. This plant growth changes the chemistry of the water and robs fish of the oxygen they need to breathe.

3 How do P and N get into water?

People add P and N to water without even knowing they're doing it. All the water that people use eventually runs into bodies of water like streams, rivers and lakes, giving P and N a free ride.

4 Where does P and N runoff come from?

Lots of places: gardens and farms using fertilizer containing P and N, city streets, dishwashing water, cars washed with soap and water in driveways. All this runs into sewers and then into lakes.

5 How do people stop the runoff that's rockin' our lakes?

Nature does it best. The more plants and trees to sop up water and slow it down, the better. The more hard surfaces like roads, the more water that flows down into the lake—even from hundreds of miles away.

6 Are subdivisions bad for lakes?

Many are because of their roads, driveways, and other hard surfaces, and because a lot of people don't understand how what they do with water hurts lakes. But the more planting there is the better. This is called LID (low-impact development).

7 So what can we do to help our lakes?

Be a champion of soft surfaces, fewer paved driveways, less lawns that need fertilizers, more plantings. You should also think about using less water and think about where water goes after you use it.

Answers
to Your Burning Questions About
the Future

What will the Great Lakes look like when we are grown up?

The Great Lakes could look completely the same or completely different or somewhere in between. What's important is that the lakes will look one way or another based on the kinds of decisions we make today.

Step into the time machine thingy and find out how!

THE TIME MACHINE THINGY

It's about time...

Let's get moving!

FAST FORWARD TO THE FUTURE!

Say we decide that it is important to take water out of lakes for drinking, and we suck the water out like a straw in our chocolate milk. Then it's possible the lakes could go dry and we could build whole cities in their place. You'd see a concrete jungle in their place in the future.

Whoa...

THE FUTURE DEPENDS ON OUR CHOICES!

Eww! No fish and no swimming. That sucks!

Say we decide that what we do on the land around lakes is a top priority, and we forget that everything we do on the land affects the water in lakes. Then the lakes might have water, but it could be murky and full of algae. When you arrived in the future, you'd see a lake that wouldn't be very good for swimming or boating. And you could forget about the fish! There wouldn't be any left.

THE TIME MACHINE THINGY

Now this is more like it! Paradise Found!

Say we remember how much we love to swim, boat, fish and skate on lakes. Then the lakes could look even better than they do now! In the future, you might see crisp, fresh waves, lots of fish and lakes with just enough boats for fun but not enough for a traffic jam!

The lakes will look the way they do depending on the choices we make!

What choices will you make?

45

ADVISORS AND CONSULTANTS
For their expert advice, we would like to thank the following people:

Janette Anderson, Great Lakes Issue Management and Reporting Section, Environment Canada; Mary Byers, author, *Rural Roots*, and *Lake Simcoe and Lake Couchiching*; Stephen Bodi, Vice President Marketing Mavea LLC; Dr. Kim Bretz, BSc, ND, Fundamentals of Health; Tracey Carrigan, York Region Environmental Services; Heidi Clelland-Sauer, MLA, Breathing Dialogues||Breathing Landscape Design, Discovery & Communications; Dr. Seanna Davidson, Monash Sustainability Institute, Monash University; Rebecca Dolson, Lake Simcoe Project Coordinator, Ministry of Natural Resources and Forestry, Aurora District; Dr. Cynthia Wesley-Esquimaux, Ph.D., Chippewa of Georgina Island, Vice Provost Lakehead University, Thunder Bay; Judy Gilchrist, Environmental Communications Specialist; Dr. Brian Ginn, Lake Simcoe Region Conservation Authority; Paul Harpley, B.Sc. (Hons.), M.A., The Zephyr Society of Lake Simcoe; John Hicks, Landscape Architect, B.L.A., ChemTech Ryerson, author; Wendy Kemp, York Region Environmental Services; Lionel Koffler, President, Firefly Books; Gabrielle Liddle, Lake Simcoe Management Biologist, Ministry of Natural Resources and Forestry, Aurora District; Claire Malcomson, Rescue Lake Simcoe Coalition Past President, Lake Simcoe Coordinating Committee member; Greg Mayne, Great Lakes Issue Management and Reporting Section, Environment Canada; Pat Prevost, Post-Graduate Certificate, Aquaculture, Fleming College; Wil Wegman, Resource Management Technician; Ontario Ministry of Natural Resources and Forestry, Aurora District; Mike Williams, Conservation Programs Specialist, Ducks Unlimited Canada; Anna van Maris, President, Parklane Nurseries Limited; Hilary Van Welter, Change Strategist, CEO Ascentia, Director ReWilding Lake Simcoe.

CREDITS

Front Cover	Collage by Deryk Ouseley
Back Cover	Photo by Krista LaChapelle
P. 4	Photo by Krista LaChapelle
P. 5	Fish in water photo by Josefa Holland–Merten C.C.; Flag photo by Krista LaChapelle
P. 6-7	Photo by Justin Leibow C.C.
P. 8	Photo by Martin St. Amant C.C.
P. 9	Great Lakes from space by NASA/Goddard SFC C.C.
P. 10	Photo by Krista LaChapelle
P. 11	Glass of snow photo by Zeevveez C.C.; Boy photo by FMSC C.C.; Leaking tap photo by Img-Buddy C.C.; Drinking fountain photo by Darwin Bell C.C.;
P. 12-13	Photo collage by Deryk Ouseley/Google Images C.C.
P. 14–15	Photo by Warren Lo Photography/
P. 16	Photo by Google Images C.C.
P. 17	Fish illustration by Nemo/Pixabay C.C.; Fish photo by Oakley Originals/Flickr C.C.
P. 18	Photo by Sean McGrath /Flickr C.C.
P. 19	Dead fish photo by Mr. TinDC/Flickr C.C.; Crayfish photo by John Goldsmith C.C.; Fish graphic by Deryk Ouseley
P. 20	Photo collage by Deryk Ouseley/Google Images C.C.
P. 22	Photo by Gazhoe/Imgur C.C.
P. 23	Pacu teeth top by Nisamanee Wan-moon C.C.; Pacu teeth bottom by Henrick Carl C.C.
P. 24-25	Photo collage by Deryk Ouseley/Google Images C.C.
P. 26-27	Photo by Krista LaChapelle
P. 28-29	Photo by Matthew Clark
P. 30-31	Photo by Patryk Sobczak
P. 32	Main photo by Krista LaChapelle; Zebra mussel photo by Google Images C.C.
P. 33	Photo by Ladies of the Lake/Annabel Slaight
P. 34	Photo by Krista LaChapelle
P. 35	Photos by Krista LaChapelle
P. 37	Beaver photo by Finch-Lake2000 C.C.; Cat photo by Ilkerender C.C.; Zebra mussel photo by United States Geological Survey/Public Domain
P. 38	Photo by Wiki/Creator Unknown C.C.
P. 39	Pacific viper fish photo by David Csepp; Fangtooth photo by Citron; Vampire squid photo by Anne-Lise Heinrichs; Diver and Anglerfish Collage by Deryk Ouseley/ CG Arena
P. 40-41	Beach pollution photo collage by Deryk Ouseley; Motor photo by Unknown/Google Images C.C.; Boat photo by John Leffmann C.C.; Soap bubbles photo by Unknown/Google Images C.C.
P. 42	Dead fish photo by U.S Environmental Protection Agency/Public Domain
P. 43	Photo Collage by Deryk Ouseley/Google Images C.C.
P. 44	Photo by Krista LaChapelle
P. 45	Collage by Deryk Ouseley/Google Images C.C.